What do we think about

Animal Welfare?

Jillian Powell

HODDER
Wayland

an imprint of Hodder Children's Books

Titles in the series

What do we think about ...

**Adoption • Alcohol • Animal Welfare • Bullying
Death • Disability • Drugs • Family Break-Up
Our Environment • Racism**

**All Wayland books encourage children to read and help
them improve their literacy.**

✓ The contents page, page numbers, headings and index
help locate specific pieces of information.

✓ The glossary reinforces alphabetic knowledge and
extends vocabulary.

✓ The further information section suggests other books
dealing with the same subject.

✓ See page 31 for ways in which you can use this book to
encourage literacy skills.

Editor: Elizabeth Gogerly
Consultant: John Bennett
Cover designer: Jan Sterling
Designer: Jean Wheeler
Photo researcher: Gina Brown
Production controller: Carol Titchener

First published in Great Britain in 1999 by
Wayland (Publishers) Ltd
Reprinted in 2002 by Hodder Wayland,
an imprint of Hodder Children's Books

© Hodder Wayland 1999

British Library Cataloguing in Publication Data

Powell, Jillian
What do we think about animal welfare?
1. Animal rights - Juvenile literature
I. Title II. Animal welfare
179.3

ISBN 0 7502 4114 4

Printed and bound in Hong Kong

Picture acknowledgements
Sylvia Cordaiy/ Humphrey Evans *cover*
(background)/ Nigel Rolstone 23 (top);
Chris Fairclough 13, 21; Angela Hampton
4, 7 (right), 9, 14, 17, 19, 27; Robert
Harding 8, 16, 20 (top)/ Jean Brooks 22;
Popperfoto 18; RSPCA/ Mark Votier
imprint/ Angela Hampton 4/ Colin Seddon
7 (left)/ 10, left, right)/ Alban Donohoe 11/
20 (bottom); Tony Stone 5, 12, 23 (bottom),
24 (top, bottom), 25, 26; Wayland *cover*
(main), *contents*, 6, 15, 28 (top), 29 (top,
bottom), 32
The publisher would like to thank the
Belmont Country Club, London NW7 and
Sainsbury's at Liphook. We would also like
to thank Marc, Ben and Tiffany Taylor.

Contents

How do we treat animals?

We share our world with many different animals. Like us, animals need food, water and a place to live. Some animals need to be cared for by us.

Animals can be our pets. They can also be kept on farms or zoos. Animals can be used by us for sports, such as horse-racing. But animals are sometimes killed for their fur. Some people think it is wrong to use animals like this.

What can we do to help look after animals?

Is it good to keep pets?

Many people like to keep pets. Pets need us to love and care for them and they give us their love back. Playing with a pet or stroking it can make us feel happy.

We can sometimes choose a pet from an animal rescue home rather than a pet shop. This means we can look after an animal which has not been cared for in the past, or is unwanted by its owner.

Richard and his family chose their dog from a Dogs' Rescue Home.

How can we care for pets?

When we keep a pet, we must learn how to care for it properly. All pets need clean homes. They need food and water every day. Some pets need plenty of space and exercise.

Some pets need to be bathed and to have their coats brushed or combed. Old or sick animals and very young animals need special care. If animals are sick, we must take them to a vet.

Sam has a goldfish. He makes sure he feeds it every day. He also cleans the bowl out every week.

Why do some people harm animals?

Sometimes, people do not know how to look after animals properly. They may not give their pets enough space and exercise, or feed them properly.

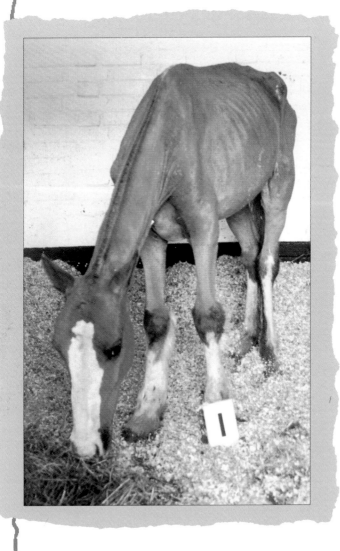

Some people even treat animals cruelly.

We can help by learning more about animals. We could also join animal welfare groups.

Charlotte's class is listening to a talk by an animal welfare officer.

What about farm animals?

Many farm animals today are kept on factory farms. They may spend their whole life indoors in cages or sheds.

Many people think this is wrong. They think animals should be kept in fields where they are free to walk around and feed. This is called free range farming.

We can help by choosing to buy meat and eggs that are produced on free range farms.

Liam is helping his dad choose free range eggs from the supermarket. They look for the free range label.

Should we kill animals for food?

Some people believe it is wrong to kill animals for food. Vegetarians don't eat any meat. Vegans don't eat meat, eggs or any food from animals.

Some people think it is all right to eat meat as long as the animals are cared for properly.

We can choose to be vegetarians if we don't want to eat any meat.

Meena and her family are vegetarian. Meena's mum knows lots of good recipes which don't use any meat.

Should we test drugs and cosmetics on animals?

Animals are used to test the safety of new drugs before they are used on people. Animals are also used to test cosmetics like shampoo and face creams.

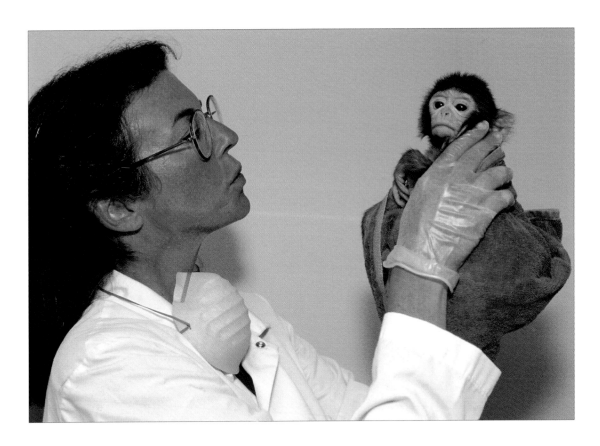

Many people think this is wrong and there is no need to use animals for tests.

We can help by choosing products which have not been tested on animals. Tess is using shampoo which has not been tested on animals. The label on the bottle says it was not tested on animals.

Should we use animals for sport?

Animals are used for sports such as horse-racing, dog-racing and fox-hunting. Some people think these sports should be stopped because they are cruel.

Other people think sports like hunting are part of country life. They say hunters kill animals, such as foxes, to stop them killing farm animals.

We can help by joining animal welfare groups. They work to prevent cruelty and rescue animals who are endangered by us.

Should we use animals for entertainment?

In some countries, animals are used for entertainment and circuses. In Spain, bull-fighting is still very popular.

Other countries allow street entertainers to keep animals like monkeys and bears. Many people think it is cruel to use animals in this way.

We can watch wildlife films and videos of animals. These entertain us without harming animals.

Josh and Louise like watching wildlife films with their family.

Should animals be kept in zoos?

People can learn a lot about animals by visiting a zoo. Today many zoos have plenty of open space for the animals. Some zoos help to save endangered animals by breeding them, then returning them to the wild.

Some people think it is wrong to keep animals in zoos. Animals kept in cages may feel bored and lonely.

The animals at this zoo are cared for properly. These polar bears can swim in a large pool. At zoos like this we can learn more about the animals and how they live.

Why are some animals endangered?

Many wild animals have died out. This is because they have been hunted for their skins, ivory, bone or other animal products.

Animals can also be endangered when their habitat is destroyed by people taking land to build new roads and towns.

We can help by joining conservation groups. We can also try to make our own wildlife habitats by planting wildflowers or making a pond.

Sharing our world

We share our world with many different living things, including birds, reptiles, fish and minibeasts, such as insects and spiders.

We must learn to care for all other animals and their habitats.

We can all help to protect animals by caring for our own pets and learning about other animals and their needs.

Notes for parents and teachers

Read this book with children one to one or in groups. Ask them what they understand by 'animal welfare'. They should understand that all living creatures have the right to live, and they share with us basic needs such as enough clean water, food and their own habitat.

The children could be asked to write an animals' charter. This could inspire creative work such as poems written from an animal's point of view.

Talk to the children about caring for pets. They should understand that different animals have different requirements of food, space and exercise. They could be encouraged to talk about how they care for their own pets or classroom pets. It may be possible to invite an animal welfare officer to the school to talk to the children.

Children could be asked to discuss topics such as animals used in sport. They could be asked to give different views for and against hunting or racing, then vote as a group to find out the majority view.

Talk about endangered species like pandas, tigers, elephants and some kinds of rhinoceros. Explain why these animals are endangered but also talk about positive initiatives such as protected species, zoo breeding schemes and wildlife reserves. Explain what we mean by "extinct" and give examples of extinct species like the dodo.

The children could visit a local zoo or nature park. Sometimes, it is possible to sponsor an animal and this could

be used to develop verbal and written skills in observation, as well as creative writing and art work.

Children could be encouraged to create their own wildlife area or pond, which could be used for scientific observation and creative work.

Glossary

animal welfare groups People who try to stop cruelty to animals and care for sick and unwanted animals.

conservation groups People who try to stop the destruction of nature and the countryside by other people.

drugs Medicine or pills which are used to fight illness and disease.

endangered When a type of animal is in danger of dying out.

factory farms Farms where animals are kept in cages or sheds.

habitat The place where an animal lives and finds its food.

ivory Elephant tusks.

Further information

Books to read

Caring for your Pets by Jillian Powell (Wayland, 1997)

Pets by Michaela Miller (Heinemann/RSPCA, 1997)

What is it like to be a baby elephant? by Honor Head
(Belitha Press, 1998)

Organizations to contact

Royal Society for the Prevention of Cruelty to Animals
(RSPCA)
Causeway, Horsham, West Sussex RH12 1HG

World Society for the Protection of Animals (WSPA)
2 Langley Lane, London SW8 1TJ

Use this book for teaching literacy

This book can help you in the literacy hour in the following ways:

✓ Children can discuss the themes and link them to their own
experiences of cruelty to animals or caring for animals' welfare.

✓ They can discuss the situations and speculate about how they might
behave in each situation.

✓ They can compare this book with fictional stories about animals and
pets to show how similar information can be presented in different ways.

✓ They can try rewriting some of the situations described in the form
of a story.

Index

Numbers in **bold** refer to pictures as well as text.